How to use the English/Spanish language option

When you insert your DVD into a DVD player, it will
automatically play in English. To play your DVD in
Spanish, go to the Main Menu and select the word "On"
next to the word "Spanish."

To return to English, use your remote and select the
word "Off" next to the word "Spanish."

CE

Published by Reader's Digest Children's Books
Reader's Digest Road, Pleasantville, NY U.S.A. 10570-7000
and Reader's Digest Children's Publishing Limited,
The Ice House, 124-126 Walcot Street, Bath UK BA1 5BG
Copyright © 2007 Reader's Digest Children's Publishing, Inc.
All rights reserved. Reader's Digest Children's Books,
the Pegasus logo, and Reader's Digest are all registered
trademarks of The Reader's Digest Association, Inc.
Book Manufactured in China.
DVD Manufactured in Hong Kong.
Conforms to ASTM F963-03 and EN 71
10 9 8 7 6 5 4 3 2 1

Ocean Life

From A to Z

Featuring the Photography of Annie Crawley

Reader's Digest
Children's Books®

Pleasantville, New York • Montréal, Québec • Bath, United Kingdom

Abalone

An abalone is a type of marine snail. There are over 70 different types of abalone! The outside shell of an abalone is rough and brown, but the inside shell is used to make mother-of-pearl.

Right: Close-up of an abalone's eye stalks

Anthias

Anthias fish are found in large numbers on coral reefs, and usually are pink, yellow, or orange. They often stay in groups of 2 to 15, but can swarm in the thousands. Imagine lots and lots of these beautiful fish swimming by you on the reef— how exciting!

Background: Anthias swarm over a coral reef.

Anemone Fish

If you saw *Finding Nemo*, you probably recognize this creature! There are different kinds of anemone fish, and some of these are called clown fish. These fish make their homes in sea anemones. The anemone fish isn't bothered by the sea anemone's stinging tentacles, but most other fish stay away. This keeps the anemone fish safe!

Above and Background: Anemone fish

B

Butterflyfish

Heads or tails? It can be hard to tell with many kinds of butterflyfish. Most of these fish have dark bands running over their eyes and dark spots or markings on their bodies. The markings can confuse a predator and give a butterflyfish time to escape being someone's lunch.

Right: Blacklip butterflyfish

Brittle Star

This creature has interesting eating habits! First, the brittle star shoves food in its mouth with all its arms. Then it chews using five jaw parts before food moves to its stomach. Brittle stars hide on coral reefs during the day and mainly come out at night.

Right: A smooth brittle star lays her eggs.

Barracuda

Barracudas can be found in huge schools, though some kinds, like the giant barracuda, prefer to hunt alone. The barracuda has been nicknamed the "Tiger of the Sea" because it hunts at night, attacks swiftly, and has a mouth full of sharp teeth.

Left and Background: Some barracuda swim in schools with as many as 1,000 other fish.

Below: Giant barracuda

C

Crab

What has 10 legs, can walk sideways, and loves leftovers? The answer is any of the 4,500 kinds of crabs. Most crabs dine on bits of plants or animals left by other animals. A crab has a hard outer shell that protects its soft body.

Right: Sally lightfoot crab

Crinoid

Also called "feather stars" or "sea lilies," crinoids may look like plants, but they are really animals. Some crinoids have as many as 200 arms that they use to catch plankton that floats by.

Right: Crinoid

Cowrie

In the past, the beautiful shell of the cowrie was used as money by some cultures. It's also been used for jewelry. Cowries are actually made by marine snails, who live inside the shells.

Left: Pair of Flamingo tongue cowries

Coral

Although they look like rocks or plants, corals are really tiny animals. A single coral animal is called a polyp. Coral polyps live together in large groups, called colonies. A colony can have millions of coral animals. There are two main types of coral: soft and hard. Hard corals can form coral reefs, which can grow quite large—the Great Barrier Reef in Australia is over 1,250 miles long!

Background: Soft coral

Cardinalfish

These coral-reef dwellers have an interesting way of producing young: the father holds the eggs in his mouth until the eggs are ready to hatch!

Above: Banggai cardinalfish

D

Dolphin

There are over 30 types of dolphins in the world's oceans. Dolphins are marine mammals, which means they breathe air, are warm blooded, and have a few other things in common with people, who are also mammals.

Right and Background: Bottlenose dolphins

Damselfish

Dad is on duty! When the female damselfish lays her eggs, the male damselfish keeps an eye on the nest until the babies are born.

Left: Garibaldi, the largest fish in the damselfish family

Below: Sergeant major damselfish

Eggs

Most marine creatures lay eggs to produce young. Some fish build nests and guard their eggs, while others simply lay their eggs and let them float in the water or sink to the bottom. Eggs come in all sizes. Some are so small they can hardly be seen!

Background: An anemone fish watches over its eggs.

Below: Nudibranch eggs form spirals or wreath shapes.

Eel

Their long, muscular bodies make eels look like snakes, but these animals are really bony fish. Eels may also look frightening because their teeth are always showing. But saltwater eels need to keep their mouths open in order to breathe. Eels are also unusual in another way—many of them can swim backward into a reef!

Above and Left: These moray eels both show some sharp teeth.

Above: White-margined moray eel

Right: Blue ribbon eel

Below: An eel is "cleaned" by a shrimp. The shrimp removes dead skin and bacteria from the eel.

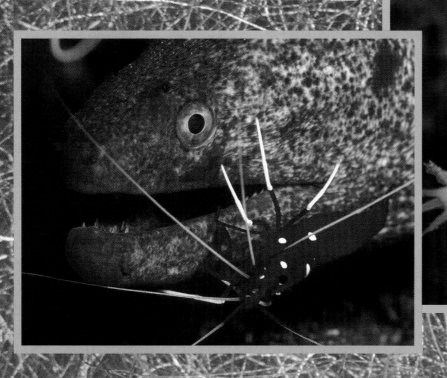

F

Filefish

Usually the scales of fish are smooth, but the scales of a filefish are rough, like sandpaper or a nail file. Closely related to triggerfish, the generally shy filefish has a long, thin spine along the top of its head.

Right: Tasseled filefish

Flathead Fish

These fish spend their entire lives on the ocean floor. When a flathead is hidden in the sand, it's almost impossible to see! Flatheads blend into their surroundings to hide from predators. This is called camouflage.

Left: The crocodile fish is a type of flathead fish.

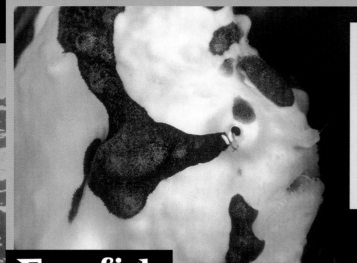

Frogfish

Frogfish are not very pretty, but these lumpy, bumpy fish are very good at hiding. They may look like rocks, sand, coral, or plants—it all depends on where the frogfish lives. And because they are so hard to spot, frogfish are great predators!

Clockwise from top: A painted frogfish, a juvenile frogfish; a warty frogfish; a painted frogfish; and a hairy frogfish

Goatfish

On land, goats are known for eating almost anything. Under the sea, goatfish are known for eating whatever they can find as they stir up the sandy ocean bottom.

Right and Background: Goatfish

Goby

The goby family is one of the biggest fish families, but it also has some of the smallest members. Most gobies are less than four inches in length. Of the many different types of gobies, one of the most interesting is the cleaner goby. These small fish form "cleaning stations" and eat the parasites from larger fish.

Below: Catalina goby

Hawkfish

Hawkfish use the fins on the sides of their bodies, called pectoral fins, to perch on top of coral. From this post, they try to spot food— just like a bird sitting in a tree does.

Left: Longnose hawkfish

Iguana

Marine iguanas are closely related to iguanas that spend all their time on land. But marine iguanas are great swimmers—they crawl into the sea to look for algae, and have been known to hold their breath for over an hour when they dive. Since iguanas are cold-blooded creatures, they must return to shore after a swim to warm up in the sun.

Above: The white substance above the nose of the marine iguana is actually salt, which the iguana blows out of its nose.

Jellyfish

These creatures are not really fish, and they don't have a single bone in their bodies. But most jellies do have many tentacles hanging from their bodies. These flexible, armlike branches allow the jelly to sting its prey. The tentacles also protect the jellyfish from predators.

Right: Upside down jellyfish

Juvenile fish

When some fish hatch from their eggs, they look like tiny versions of their parents. But some fish must go through many changes before they look like adults.

Left: Juvenile filefish

Jacks

Like many fish, jacks swim together in groups called schools. Jacks swim together for safety. They also work together in a pack to hunt other fish to eat.

Background: Jacks

Kelpfish

As their name implies, most kelpfish live near kelp forests, though some may live in eel grass beds. The long, thin body of a kelpfish helps it swim through the plants with ease. This fish is also colored red, green, or brown to blend with its surroundings—and some kelpfish can even change color.

Left: Juvenile giant kelpfish

Kelp

Kelp forests are important homes, or habitats, for many kinds of fish, marine mammals, and other creatures. For example, the sea otter will wrap itself in kelp fronds when it sleeps in the water—not because the otter is cold, but because the otter doesn't want to drift away. Like all algae, kelp needs sunlight to grow—and some kelp has been known to grow as high as 200 feet tall. The air-filled sacs attached to the kelp leaves help it reach the surface, where the algae can get sunlight.

Background: A kelp forest

Lobster

Like crabs, the soft bodies of lobsters are covered in hard shells. To grow, the lobster must shed its shell, a process called molting. In its first five to seven years, a lobster may molt as many as 25 times, until it weighs about one pound. After that, a lobster usually molts about once a year.

Left: Hairy squat lobster

Above: Caribbean reef lobster

Lionfish

This fish may be one of the most spectacular-looking in the ocean, but it is also one of the most dangerous. A lionfish has as many as 18 long, sharp poisonous spines.

Left: Lionfish

Mackerel

There are a number of fish that belong to the mackerel family. They are fast-swimming predators that live in the open ocean. Most mackerels migrate, or travel, as the ocean temperature changes.

Left: King mackerel

Mussel

A mussel is a bivalve. Its top and bottom shell are connected by a hinge. Mussels are mostly found on the ocean bottom, where they are harvested for food. Sometimes they are found attached to rocks or stuck to boats. Mussels are filter feeders. This means they take in seawater and strain, or filter, food from the water. They also get oxygen this way.

Below: Mussel

Mandarin Fish

The crazy colors and wild patterns on a Mandarin fish make it very unusual. Wavy lines and swirls in blue, orange, green, or yellow can help it blend into a colorful coral reef.

Above: Mandarin fish

N

Nudibranch

Most people think slugs are ugly and slimy. But nudibranchs, which are sea slugs, are often quite pretty and colorful. Unlike snails, nudibranchs don't have hard shells to protect their soft bodies. Instead, their bright colors help to protect them. Some nudibranchs use their colors to hide from predators. For others, the bright colors warn predators that the nudibranch is poisonous.

Top: Banana nudibranch

Right: Navanax

Below: Chromodoris

Background: Nudibranch on soft coral

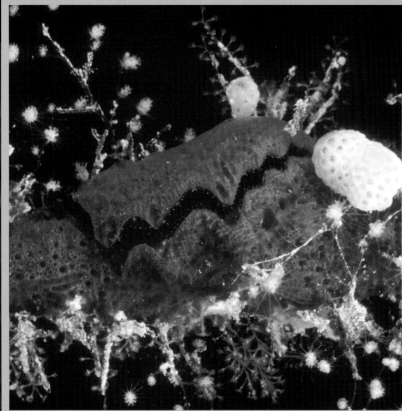

Oyster

Oysters are probably best known for making pearls, though not all oysters produce pearls. When a grain of sand gets into an oyster's shell, the oyster coats the sand with layers of a special substance called "nacre". Over many years this process forms a pearl.

Left: Oyster

Octopus

An octopus has two rows of suction cups along each of its eight arms. These suction cups help the octopus get a good grip on favorite foods like crabs. An octopus can also be a quick change artist—when it moves around the ocean, its coloring changes to blend in with its new surroundings.

Left: Octopus luteus

Above: Walking octopus

P

Pipefish

These unusual-looking creatures have long, slim bodies that blend with their surroundings. But some members of the pipefish family are unusual in other ways—like the male seahorses that carry the eggs until they hatch. When the juvenile pipefish are born, they need to learn to swim away quickly, because some pipefish will eat their young.

Above and Right: Ornate ghost pipefish

Parrotfish

This fish gets its name because its teeth resemble the beak of a parrot. The parrotfish uses its teeth to scrape algae from rocks and coral. Parrotfish are very important to the ocean ecosystem. By eating algae, they prevent plants from becoming overgrown and choking coral. When they eat coral along with algae, the coral moves through their bodies and is ground into sand.

Left: Parrotfish

Queen Conch

The queen conch (pronounced "konk") is actually a marine snail. It is known for its beautiful shell, which reaches its full size when the queen conch is about 3 years old. Most of these animals can live for 20 to 30 years if left undisturbed, but they are a favorite food of sea turtles, eagle rays, other conches, and humans.

Background: Queen conch

Below: Queen conch's eye

R

Ray

The skeleton of a ray is made of a tough substance called cartilage—if you feel the rubbery end of your nose, you'll know what cartilage feels like. All rays have long tails and flattened bodies, but they come in different shapes, sizes, and colors. While most rays have sharp spines or stingers on the ends of their tails, divers usually have nothing to fear from these gentle creatures.

Above: Blue spotted stingray

Background: Southern stingray

Razorfish

A person might get a headache if they stood on their head all day, but the razorfish doesn't seem to mind. Razorfish feed with their heads facing down, and they can even swim in this up-and-down position. They are usually found in small groups hiding among coral.

Below: Razorfish

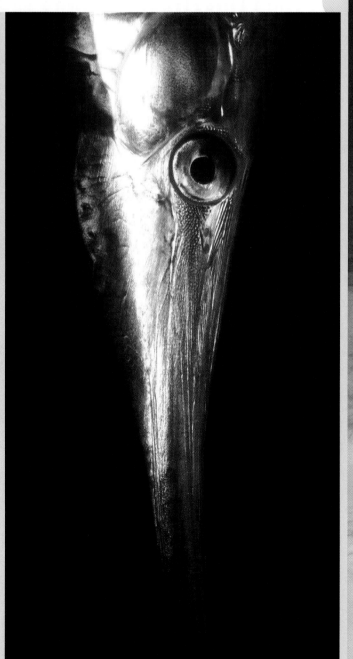

Remora

Also known as suckerfish, remoras are hitchhikers in the ocean world. A remora attaches itself to sharks, whales, or other larger animals by using a sucking disk on the top of its head. This doesn't bother the host animal, and the remora gets a free ride, and perhaps bits of food left behind from its host.

Above: Remoras

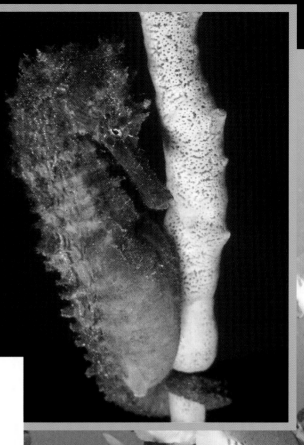

Seahorse

They may not look like it, but seahorses are actually fish. Their curved heads and long, narrow snouts help seahorses suck up tiny animals living in the coral reef.

Above Left: Pink pygmy seahorse

Above Right: Seahorse

Surgeonfish

Surgeonfish have spines on either side of their tails. These spines are sharp, like a surgeon's knife or scalpel. These colorful fish usually eat algae that they scrape off of rocks with their bristly teeth.

Background: Surgeonfish

Sponges

A sponge gets food by taking in seawater through tiny holes called pores—which cover the sponge's body. After the sponge removes its food from the water, it pushes the water out through other openings in its body.

Background: Red rope sponge

Sea Lion

These marine mammals are good swimmers. Like all mammals, sea lions need to breathe air. But they can stay underwater for up to 40 minutes to look for fish, squid, or crabs to eat. A thick layer of fat, called blubber, helps keep them warm.

Above: Sea lion

Snail

Marine snails grow hard shells that come in all sort of shapes, sizes, and colors. The hard shell protects the snail's soft body.

Left: Purple top snail

Sea Star

You probably recognize these creatures—which you may know as starfish. Each of the sea star's five arms is lined with suction cups, which help this creature move along the rocky ocean bottom. The sea star's strong arms also allow it to pry open a tightly closed oyster for a meal. But sometimes the sea star is another animal's dinner. If it is lucky, it might simply lose an arm. If that happens, then the sea star can grow a new one.

Top Left: Cushion sea star

Bottom Left: Orange sea star

Background: Knobby sea star

Shark

Sharks have been around for more than 300 million years. They exist in every ocean on earth.

Right: Whitetip reef shark

Background: Gray reef shark with rainbow runners

Scorpionfish

You wouldn't want to step on a member of the scorpionfish family, because the needlelike spines along the back of the fish are poisonous. In fact, one type, the stonefish, has such strong poison it can kill a person. Many of these fish blend very well into their rocky homes on the ocean floor.

Left: Bearded scorpionfish

T, U

Turtle

Sea turtles are made for life in the sea. Unlike a land turtle, a sea turtle cannot pull its flippers or head inside its shell. But its flippers make great paddles to help the turtle move through the water.

Right: Hawksbill sea turtle

Toadfish

These slow-moving fish are found in many different habitats—from coral reefs to the sandy ocean floor. Male toadfish are also able to make a humming sound that attracts female toadfish.

Above: Whitespotted toadfish

Urchin

Sea urchins are round, spiny creatures that are related to sea stars. Their spines, some of which are very sharp, protect them from predators. Still, sea urchins are a favorite food of creatures such as sea otters, so sea urchins often hide during the day and come out at night to eat. Sea urchins often eat kelp.

Background: Purple sea urchins

Vase Sponge

Some sponges can grow very large—the vase sponge is one of them. It can grow almost two feet high and three feet wide. The vase sponge takes in seawater, removes the food it finds, and then pumps out the seawater through the large opening in the center.

Left: Vase sponges

Whelk

The whelk is another kind of marine snail—and many are predators. This type of whelk uses its radula, which is a rough, tonguelike organ, to drill into the shells of prey such as lobsters, crabs, and clams.

Left: Whelks have spiral shells.

Worm

Do you think the only worms in the sea are the ones on the end of a fishing hook? Some marine worms look very different from earthworms, and can actually be quite beautiful.

Background: Feather duster worms

Xeno Crab

These crabs are often seen—or not seen—on sea whips, which are a type of coral. The crab's color matches the sea whip's color, so these small crabs are often overlooked by predators.

Above: Xeno crab

Yellow Tube Sponge

There are over 5,000 types of sponges in the world's oceans. Some, like the yellow tube sponge, are called freestanding sponges. They attach to coral or the ocean bottom, then grow upward.

Background: Yellow tube sponge

Zoanthid

Zoanthids are a type of anemone that are closely related to coral. Colorful zoanthids live in shallow waters, although less colorful ones can be found in deeper waters.

Right: A colony of zoanthids looks like a garden of flowers.